Build up your revision momentum with CGP!

There's a lot to learn for the AQA 9-1 GCSE Physics exams...
it can be tough to get off the starting blocks with your revision.

Not to worry — this brilliant CGP book is packed with Physics tests
that only take ten minutes each. So you don't have to plough through them
for hours in one session, just fit one in whenever you have a gap in your day.

Every topic from the course is covered, and answers are included at the back.
It's a great way to make sure you're on the right track for the exams!

CGP — still the best ☺

Our sole aim here at CGP is to produce the highest quality books
— carefully written, immaculately presented and
dangerously close to being funny.

Then we work our socks off to get them out to you
— at the cheapest possible prices.

Published by CGP

Editors:
Sarah Armstrong, Duncan Lindsay, Ethan Starmer-Jones, Sarah Williams

ISBN: 978 1 78294 846 9

With thanks to Glenn Rogers, Charlotte Whiteley and Mark Edwards for the proofreading.
With thanks to Emily Smith for the copyright research.

Clipart from Corel®
Illustrations by: Sandy Gardner Artist, email sandy@sandygardner.co.uk
Printed by Sterling, Kettering

Based on the classic CGP style created by Richard Parsons.

Text, design, layout and original illustrations © Coordination Group Publications Ltd. (CGP) 2017
All rights reserved.

Photocopying this book is not permitted, even if you have a CLA licence.
Extra copies are available from CGP with next day delivery • 0800 1712 712 • www.cgpbooks.co.uk

Contents

Topics for Paper 1

Test 1: Energy 2
Test 2: Energy 4
Test 3: Energy 6
Test 4: Electricity 8
Test 5: Electricity 10
Test 6: Electricity 12
Test 7: Particle Model of Matter 14
Test 8: Particle Model of Matter 16
Test 9: Atomic Structure 18
Test 10: Atomic Structure 20

Mixed Tests for Paper 1

Test 11: Paper 1 Mixed Topics 22
Test 12: Paper 1 Mixed Topics 24
Test 13: Paper 1 Mixed Topics 26
Test 14: Paper 1 Mixed Topics 28
Test 15: Paper 1 Mixed Topics 30

Topics for Paper 2

Test 16: Forces 32
Test 17: Forces 34
Test 18: Forces 36
Test 19: Waves 38
Test 20: Waves 40
Test 21: Waves 42
Test 22: Magnetism and Electromagnetism 44
Test 23: Magnetism and Electromagnetism 46
Test 24: Space Physics 48
Test 25: Space Physics 50

Mixed Tests for Paper 2

Test 26: Paper 2 Mixed Topics 52
Test 27: Paper 2 Mixed Topics 54
Test 28: Paper 2 Mixed Topics 56
Test 29: Paper 2 Mixed Topics 58
Test 30: Paper 2 Mixed Topics 60

Answers 62

Progress Chart 67

Test 1: Energy

There are **11 questions** in this test. Give yourself **10 minutes** to answer them all.

1. Which energy store is energy usefully transferred to in a blender?
   A   The kinetic energy store of the blades
   B   The elastic potential energy store of the blades
   C   The magnetic energy store of the blades
   [1]

2. The amount of energy transferred by an appliance depends on...
   A   ... its power and size.
   B   ... its power and mass.
   C   ... its power and the time it is on for.
   [1]

3. What happens to the amount of energy in a car's kinetic energy store when the car slows down?
   A   It remains the same.
   B   It decreases as some energy is transferred away to different energy stores.
   C   It decreases as some energy is destroyed.
   [1]

4. Which of these is a disadvantage of using solar cells to generate electricity?
   A   They're only reliable in sunny countries.
   B   They produce CO_2 when running.
   C   They destroy wildlife habitats.
   [1]

5. When an object falls from a height, the maximum energy transferred to its kinetic energy store is equal to...
   A   ... the energy transferred to its gravitational potential energy store.
   B   ... the energy transferred away from its gravitational potential energy store.
   [1]

6. True or False? "If a moving object doubles its speed, it doubles the energy in its kinetic energy store."
   A   True
   B   False
   [1]

7. What is the name of a system in which there is no net change in the total energy?
   A   A closed system
   B   An open system
   C   A mechanical system
   [1]

8. 800 J of energy is supplied to a toaster with an efficiency of 25%. What is the useful output of the toaster?
   A   200 J
   B   775 J
   C   1000 J
   [1]

9. A go-kart travels along a straight length of track at 8.5 m/s.
The go-kart and its driver have a combined mass of 160 kg.
Calculate the total energy in the kinetic energy stores of the go-kart and driver.

....

....

Energy = ... J
[2]

10. Describe two problems with generating electricity using nuclear power.

1. ....

....

2. ....

....
[2]

11. 2925 J of energy is needed to increase the temperature of 500 g of copper by 15 °C.

Calculate the specific heat capacity of copper.

change in thermal energy = mass × specific heat capacity × temperature change

....

....

....

....

Specific heat capacity = ... J/kg°C
[3]

15

Topics for Paper 1: Energy

Test 2: Energy

There are **11 questions** in this test. Give yourself **10 minutes** to answer them all.

1. When a racket hits a ball, energy is transferred from the racket's kinetic energy store to the ball's kinetic energy store. This energy is transferred...

   A ... by heating.

   B ... electrically.

   C ... mechanically.

   [1]

2. Which of these is a disadvantage of using wind turbines to generate electricity?

   A They can be noisy.

   B They release atmospheric pollution (CO_2) when running.

   C They produce dangerous waste that is difficult to dispose of.

   [1]

3. Electric heater A has a power rating of 1 kW. Electric heater B has a power rating of 880 W. Which transfers the most energy in 2 hours?

   A Heater A

   B Heater B

   [1]

4. True or False? "A toaster with a power of 4 W transfers 4 J of energy per minute."

   A True

   B False

   [1]

5. The rate of energy transfer from a house can be reduced by...

   A ... having walls with a low thermal conductivity.

   B ... having walls with a high thermal conductivity.

   [1]

6. Pick a suitable option that can be used to improve the efficiency of a battery-powered toy car.

   A Insulate the car.

   B Increase the input energy to the car.

   C Lubricate any moving parts in the car.

   [1]

7. When a rock rolls down a hill, some energy in its gravitational potential energy store is transferred to other stores. Which of these stores is energy **not** transferred to?

   A The rock's kinetic energy store

   B The rock's chemical energy store

   C The thermal energy store of the surroundings

   [1]

8. A cannon uses explosives to launch a ball into the air. Which is a wasteful energy transfer that occurs when the cannon is fired?

   A Chemical energy store of explosives → Kinetic energy store of ball

   B Chemical energy store of explosives → Gravitational potential energy store of ball

   C Chemical energy store of explosives → Thermal energy store of ball

   [1]

Topics for Paper 1: Energy

9. Suggest two environmental disadvantages of using tidal-powered turbines to generate electricity.

1. ....

....

2. ....

....
[2]

10. A student uses a heater to provide energy to three 0.5 kg blocks made from different materials. She measures their temperatures at regular intervals for five minutes. The graph on the right shows her results. State and explain which block of material has the highest specific heat capacity.

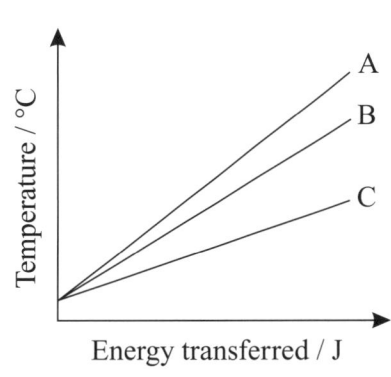

....

....
[2]

11. A robot has a power output of 50 W. How much energy does it transfer in 2 minutes?

....

....

....

Energy = ... J
[3]

15

Test 3: Energy

There are **11 questions** in this test. Give yourself **10 minutes** to answer them all.

1. Two materials with the same mass and different specific heat capacities are cooled by 10° C. Which material emits more energy?

   A The material with the higher specific heat capacity

   B The material with the lower specific heat capacity

   [1]

2. When a spring is compressed, which of these energy stores is energy transferred to?

   A The spring's elastic potential energy store

   B The spring's nuclear energy store

   C The spring's magnetic energy store

   [1]

3. Two garages of equal size and shape have walls made of the same material. One garage has thicker walls than the other. They are heated to the same temperature then left to cool. Which garage would cool the fastest?

   A The one with thick walls.

   B The one with thin walls.

   [1]

4. Power is the...

   A ... conservation of momentum.

   B ... energy of a moving object.

   C ... rate of doing work.

   [1]

5. What is the correct equation for calculating the amount of energy in an object's kinetic energy store?

   A $E_k = \frac{1}{2}mv$

   B $E_k = mv$

   C $E_k = \frac{1}{2}mv^2$

   [1]

6. Motor 1 and motor 2 each lift objects of equal weight. They both have the same power rating but motor 2 lifts the weight faster. Which motor is more efficient?

   A Motor 1

   B Motor 2

   [1]

7. We continue using non-renewable energy resources despite their negative impact on the environment. Which of the following is a possible reason for this?

   A Because non-renewable resources will never run out.

   B Because non-renewable resources are more reliable than renewable alternatives.

   C Because renewable alternatives are more harmful to the environment.

   [1]

8. 250 J of energy is supplied to a fan. The fan transfers 100 J of this energy to useful energy stores. What is the efficiency of the fan?

   A 0.1

   B 0.4

   C 0.6

   [1]

Topics for Paper 1: Energy

9. Describe the useful energy transfers in a hairdryer.

....

....

....
[2]

10. A 500 g object falls off a cliff and loses 100 J from its gravitational potential energy store. If the gravitational field strength, $g = 9.8$ N/kg, how high is the cliff?

....

....

....

Height = ... m
[3]

11. The graph below shows the temperatures of three identical flasks of water over time. They are all in the same room, and each one is wrapped in a different insulating material. State and explain which of the three materials is the best insulator.

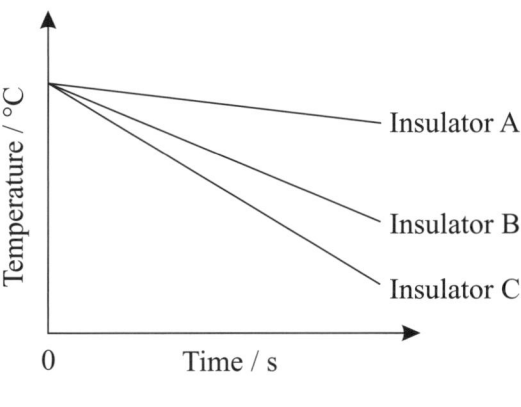

....

....
[2]

Test 4: Electricity

There are **11 questions** in this test. Give yourself **10 minutes** to answer them all.

1. True or False? "Transformers are used to carry electricity all around the country."
   A   True
   B   False
   [1]

2. True or False? "The resistance of a thermistor is higher in hot conditions than in the cold."
   A   True
   B   False
   [1]

3. Which of the following is a device that emits light?
   A   LDE
   B   LDR
   C   LED
   [1]

4. A current of 2 A passes through a device with a resistance of 8 Ω. What is the power of the device?
   A   16 W
   B   32 W
   C   128 W
   [1]

5. True or False? "Two components connected in parallel will each have the same potential difference across them."
   A   True
   B   False
   [1]

6. Static electricity is caused by the movement of which particles?
   A   Electrons
   B   Neutrons
   C   Protons
   [1]

7. In a circuit with a fixed potential difference, what would happen to the current if you increased the resistance?
   A   The current would increase.
   B   The current would stay the same.
   C   The current would decrease.
   [1]

8. Increasing the potential difference of electricity at a given power...
   A   ... increases the energy lost through heating.
   B   ... decreases the current.
   C   ... increases the rate of flow of charge.
   [1]

Topics for Paper 1: Electricity

9. A student is investigating the relationship between the length of a conductor and its resistance.

The graph on the right shows the results of her experiment.

Describe the relationship between the length of the conductor and its resistance.

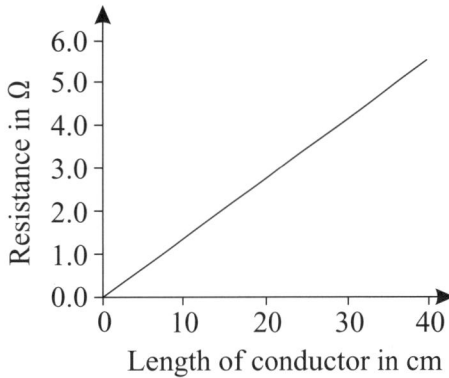

....

....
[1]

10. While in use, a 1.2 V cell transfers 5.4 kJ of energy. How much charge passed through the cell in this time?

....

....

....

Charge = ... C
[3]

11. The potential difference-current graph of a filament lamp is shown on the right.

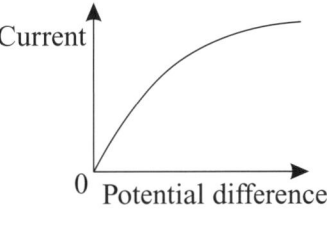

Explain why the graph curves as the current increases.

....

....

....

....
[3]

Test 5: Electricity

There are **10 questions** in this test. Give yourself **10 minutes** to answer them all.

1. What is the name for electric current that is constantly changing direction?

    A   Alternating current (ac)

    B   Direct current (dc)

    C   Switching current (sc)

    [1]

2. True or False? "Potential difference is the work done per ampere of current passing between two points."

    A   True

    B   False

    [1]

3. True or False? "A static charge can build up when two insulating materials are rubbed against each other."

    A   True

    B   False

    [1]

4. True or False? "In a series circuit, the source potential difference is shared between all components."

    A   True

    B   False

    [1]

5. True or False? "Transmitting electricity at a high potential difference and a low current is more energy efficient than transmitting at a low potential difference and a high current."

    A   True

    B   False

    [1]

6. What causes the wire inside a filament bulb to heat up when electrical charge flows through it?

    A   Earthing

    B   Insulation

    C   Resistance

    [1]

7. Electric current is...

    A   ... the driving force that pushes charges around a circuit.

    B   ... a measure of how much charges slow down as they flow through a circuit.

    C   ... the flow of electrical charge.

    [1]

8. Which wire inside a three-core cable is coated with blue plastic?

    A   Earth

    B   Live

    C   Neutral

    [1]

Topics for Paper 1: Electricity

9. The circuit diagram below shows two resistors connected in series with a battery.

Find the reading on voltmeter V_3.

....

Potential difference = ... V

Find the total resistance, R, of the circuit.

....

Resistance = ... Ω

Find the reading on the ammeter.

....

....

Current = ... A

[4]

10. The image below shows the national grid.

State the name given to the electrical devices labelled X, and describe their purpose in the national grid.

....

....

....

....

[3]

Test 6: Electricity

There are **11 questions** in this test. Give yourself **10 minutes** to answer them all.

1. True or False? "The UK mains electricity supply is direct current."

   A   True

   B   False

   [1]

2. True or False? "The current is the same at any point in a single closed loop of wire that is connected to a power supply".

   A   True

   B   False

   [1]

3. In the UK, what is the typical potential difference between the live wire and earth wire in an electrical appliance?

   A   230 V

   B   0 V

   C   12 V

   [1]

4. What type of resistor could be used in a sensing circuit designed to turn on an automatic night light when it gets too dark?

   A   diode

   B   thermistor

   C   LDR

   [1]

5. The resistance of an ohmic conductor at a constant temperature...

   A   ... is higher when larger currents flow through it.

   B   ... doesn't change as the current varies.

   C   ... is low when the current flows in one direction, but much higher when current flows in the reverse direction.

   [1]

6. Components connected in a parallel circuit will usually receive...

   A   ... a fraction of the supply potential difference.

   B   ... the same current as any other component in the circuit.

   C   ... the full supply potential difference.

   [1]

7. Resistors A and B are connected in series with a power supply.
   Resistor A has a resistance of 3 Ω.
   Resistor B has a resistance of 9 Ω.
   What is the total resistance in the circuit?

   A   6 Ω

   B   3 Ω

   C   12 Ω

   [1]

8. Adding resistors in parallel decreases the total resistance of the circuit because...

   A   ... it increases the total current that can flow around the circuit.

   B   ... it decreases the potential difference through the circuit.

   C   ... it decreases the charge that can flow through the circuit.

   [1]

Topics for Paper 1: Electricity

9. Sketch the electric field around the negatively charged sphere shown below.

[2]

10. Describe how static charge is built up when two insulating materials are rubbed together.

....

....

....

....
[2]

11. Hair straighteners with a power of 150 W are plugged into a 230 V mains supply. Calculate the current through the hair straighteners.

....

....

....

....

Current = ... A
[3]

Test 7: Particle Model of Matter

There are **11 questions** in this test. Give yourself **10 minutes** to answer them all.

1. True or False? "Liquids are generally denser than solids and gases."

   A   True
   B   False
   [1]

2. What are the units for density?

   A kg/m^2
   B kg/m^3
   C m^3/kg
   [1]

3. What happens to the pressure of a gas held at constant temperature when the volume it occupies is halved?

   A   It doubles
   B   It halves
   C   It stays the same
   [1]

4. The internal energy of a system is equal to...

   A   ... the total energy that its particles have in their kinetic energy stores.
   B   ... the total energy that its particles have in their potential energy stores.
   C   ... the total energy that its particles have in their kinetic and potential energy stores.
   [1]

5. Which of the following is not caused by increasing the energy of the particles in a liquid?

   A   Increase in temperature
   B   Boiling
   C   Condensing
   [1]

6. True or False? "The particles in a solid are held closely together in an irregular arrangement."

   A   True
   B   False
   [1]

7. What happens to the mass of a substance when it changes from a solid to a liquid?

   A   It increases
   B   It decreases
   C   It stays the same
   [1]

8. What quantity gives the energy released when 1 kg of a liquid becomes a solid with no change in temperature?

   A   Specific latent heat of vaporisation
   B   Specific latent heat of fusion
   C   Specific heat capacity
   [1]

Topics for Paper 1: Particle Model of Matter

9. Describe how the arrangement of particles in a solid is different to the arrangement of particles in a gas.

   ....

   ....
   [1]

10. Ethanol has a specific latent heat of vaporisation of 855 kJ/kg.
    Calculate the energy required to boil 0.60 kg of ethanol.

    thermal energy for a change of state = mass × specific latent heat

    ....

    ....

    ....

    Energy = ... J
    [3]

11. Explain why a bicycle tyre feels warmer after being inflated with a pump.

    ....

    ....

    ....

    ....
    [3]

Test 8: Particle Model of Matter

There are **11 questions** in this test. Give yourself **10 minutes** to answer them all.

1. True or False? "Doing work on a gas decreases the internal energy of the gas."

   A   True

   B   False

   [1]

2. True or False? "The temperature of a gas is related to the average energy in the kinetic energy stores of its particles."

   A   True

   B   False

   [1]

3. Changes of state are different to chemical changes because...

   A   ... changes of state can be reversed to recover the original properties of the material.

   B   ... changes of state result in the creation of new substances.

   C   ... changes of state cannot happen to gases.

   [1]

4. What is the specific heat capacity of a substance?

   A   The energy released by a substance when it freezes.

   B   The total energy stored by the particles in a system.

   C   The energy needed to raise the temperature of 1 kg of a substance by 1°C.

   [1]

5. Which of the following statements about gas particles is **not** true?

   A   Gas particles travel at high speeds.

   B   Gas particles travel in random directions.

   C   Gas particles have less energy than liquid and solid particles.

   [1]

6. What is the specific latent heat of fusion?

   A   The amount of energy needed to melt 1 kg of a substance.

   B   The amount of energy needed to boil 1 kg of a substance.

   C   The amount of energy needed to condense 1 kg of a substance.

   [1]

7. In which direction does the pressure of a gas in a container produce a net force?

   A   At right angles to the walls of the container

   B   Parallel to the walls of the container

   C   Directly upwards

   [1]

8. What will happen to the pressure of a fixed volume of gas if its temperature is increased?

   A   It will decrease

   B   It will increase

   C   It will stay the same

   [1]

Topics for Paper 1: Particle Model of Matter

9. A temperature-time graph for a substance that is being cooled down is shown below. Identify the state of the substance at point X.

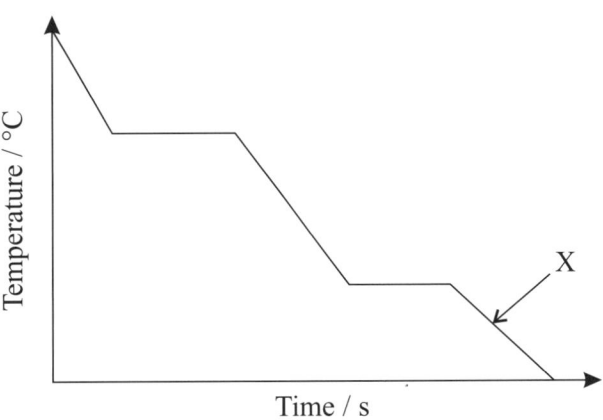

State = ...
[1]

10. A piece of gold has a volume of 2.00×10^{-5} m³ and a mass of 0.386 kg. Calculate the density of gold.

....

....

Density = ... kg/m³
[2]

11. Describe how the density of a solid object of known mass can be measured using a eureka can.

....

....

....

....

....
[4]

Test 9: Atomic Structure

There are **12 questions** in this test. Give yourself **10 minutes** to answer them all.

1. True or False? "People living in different parts of the UK will be exposed to different amounts of background radiation."

   A True

   B False

   [1]

2. What particle can trigger nuclear fission when it is absorbed by a uranium nucleus?

   A Electron

   B Proton

   C Neutron

   [1]

3. Which of these is the most dangerous outside the body?

   A Alpha radiation

   B Beta and gamma radiation

   C All types of radiation are equally dangerous.

   [1]

4. What is the name for atoms with the same number of protons but different numbers of neutrons?

   A Ions

   B Isomers

   C Isotopes

   [1]

5. True or False? "The results of the alpha scattering experiment led to the development of the plum pudding model of the atom."

   A True

   B False

   [1]

6. The count rate of a radioactive sample falls from 130 Bq to 65 Bq in 15 minutes. What is its half-life?

   A 15 minutes

   B 30 minutes

   C 1 hour

   [1]

7. What is it called when two small nuclei join together?

   A Fusion

   B Fission

   [1]

8. True or False? "Any exposure to ionising radiation will kill living cells."

   A True

   B False

   [1]

Topics for Paper 1: Atomic Structure

9. What is the difference between an atom and an ion?

   ....

   ....
   [1]

10. The decay of phosphorus-32 is shown below.

    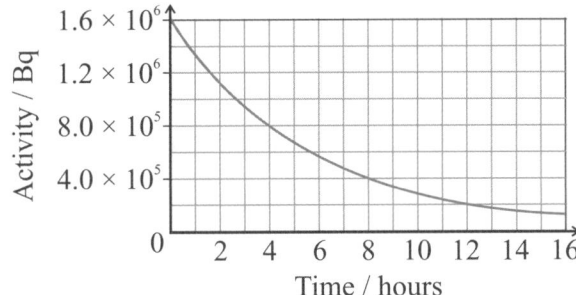

    Complete the equation by writing in the missing atomic number and mass number of the product.
    [2]

11. Use this graph to work out the half-life of the radioactive sample.

    Half-life = ... hours
    [2]

12. Describe the difference between irradiation and contamination.

    ....

    ....

    ....
    [2]

Test 10: Atomic Structure

There are **11 questions** in this test. Give yourself **10 minutes** to answer them all.

1. True or False? "The longer the half-life of a radioactive sample, the sooner it will stop being radioactive."

   A True

   B False

   [1]

2. True or False? "When a radioactive nucleus emits a beta particle, its atomic number increases."

   A True

   B False

   [1]

3. True or False? "The plum pudding model suggested that an atom was a sphere of positively charged mass with small negative electrons stuck in it."

   A True

   B False

   [1]

4. Which type of radiation can penetrate the furthest into materials?

   A Alpha

   B Beta

   C Gamma

   [1]

5. Which of these statements is correct?

   A Background radiation is around us all the time.

   B People must be shielded from all background radiation.

   C Background radiation is only caused by fallout from nuclear weapons tests.

   [1]

6. Which type of radiation is the same as a helium nucleus?

   A Alpha

   B Beta

   C Gamma

   [1]

7. True or False? "When an atom is ionised it always gains an overall negative charge."

   A True

   B False

   [1]

8. Which of the following gives the number of neutrons in the nucleus of an atom?

   A The mass number

   B The mass number – the atomic number

   C The mass number + the atomic number

   [1]

Topics for Paper 1: Atomic Structure

9. A radioactive sample has a count rate of 960 Bq. Its half-life is 30 minutes.
    How long will it take for the count rate to drop to 120 Bq?

    ....

    ....

    ....

    Time = ... minutes
    [2]

10. Describe how the orbit of an electron around an atom's nucleus
    changes when the electron absorbs an electromagnetic wave.

    ....

    ....

    ....
    [2]

11. Nuclear reactors are powered by a controlled chain reaction.
    Describe how nuclear fission can cause a chain reaction.

    ....

    ....

    ....

    ....
    [3]

Topics for Paper 1: Atomic Structure

Test 11: Paper 1 Mixed Topics

There are **11 questions** in this test. Give yourself **10 minutes** to answer them all.

1. The amount of energy needed to raise the temperature of 1 kg of a substance by 1 °C is...

   A ... its boiling point.

   B ... its specific heat capacity.

   C ... its change in heat capacity.

   [1]

2. True or False? "A live wire can still be dangerous even when a switch in the mains circuit is open."

   A True

   B False

   [1]

3. Which of the following is used in fission reactors?

   A Uranium

   B Hydrogen

   C Helium

   [1]

4. True or False? "The atomic number of an alpha particle is 4."

   A True

   B False

   [1]

5. What is the power of a device that transfers 20 J in five seconds?

   A 4 W

   B 20 W

   C 100 W

   [1]

6. True or False? "If a resistor is added to a circuit in parallel, the total resistance of the circuit will increase."

   A True

   B False

   [1]

7. Which of the following equations correctly shows the relationship between the energy in an object's gravitational potential energy store (E_p), the object's mass (m), the gravitational field strength (g) and the object's height (h)?

   A $E_p = m \times g \times h$

   B $E_p = (m \times g) \div h$

   C $E_p = m \div (g \times h)$

   [1]

8. Which of these is true in the nuclear model of the atom?

   A The nucleus in the atom is uncharged.

   B The atom is a ball of positive charge with electrons evenly distributed throughout.

   C The mass of the atom is concentrated at its centre.

   [1]

9. Cancer is a condition in which tissue in the body grows uncontrollably.
State why ionising radiation is used in cancer treatment and describe how it is used.

....

....

....
[2]

10. A car's headlights are switched on. The headlights are connected in parallel in an electrical circuit. One light goes out when its bulb blows.
Why don't both lights go out when one bulb blows?

....

....

....
[2]

11. The graph on the right shows the number of radioactive nuclei in an archaeological sample over time.
Use the graph to calculate the half-life of the radioactive nuclei and calculate the number of radioactive nuclei left in the sample after 16.8×10^3 years.

....

....

....

....

Half-life = ... years

Number of nuclei = ...
[3]

Test 12: Paper 1 Mixed Topics

There are **10 questions** in this test. Give yourself **10 minutes** to answer them all.

1. What happens to the resistance of a filament lamp as the temperature of the filament increases?

   A It increases

   B It decreases

   C It stays the same
   [1]

2. Which of these is not found in the nucleus of an atom?

   A Electrons

   B Neutrons

   C Protons
   [1]

3. What happens to a nucleus when it emits a gamma ray?

   A Its mass decreases

   B Its charge decreases

   C Its mass and charge remain unchanged
   [1]

4. Which of the following is equal to the efficiency of a device?

   A total power input ÷ useful power output

   B useful power output ÷ total power input

   C total power input × useful power output
   [1]

5. Which of the following correctly describes the energy source used in geothermal power?

   A Energy released from controlled nuclear fission reactions.

   B Energy released by burning plant products.

   C Energy released by hot rocks in the ground.
   [1]

6. What are the units for specific heat capacity?

   A J/kg °C

   B kg/J °C

   C °C/Jkg
   [1]

7. True or False? "The pressure of a gas held at constant volume decreases if the temperature is decreased."

   A True

   B False
   [1]

8. True or False? "After a substance is condensed, it can be sublimated to recover its original properties."

   A True

   B False
   [1]

9. A student has a source of radiation that emits one of the three types of ionising nuclear radiation. She places the source opposite a Geiger-Muller tube and detector and records the count rate. She then places a sheet of paper between the source and the detector and records the count rate, and then repeats this with a sheet of aluminium instead of paper. Describe how her results will allow her to work out which type of radiation is emitted by the source.

....

....

....

....

....
[3]

10. A circuit diagram is shown below.

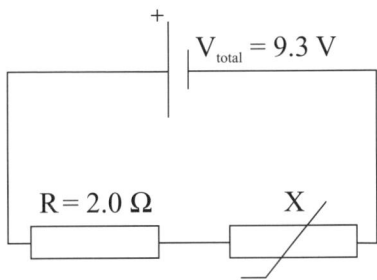

Identify component X.

....

Calculate the current passing through the circuit when component X has a resistance of 3.0 Ω.

....

....

....

Current = ... A
[4]

Test 13: Paper 1 Mixed Topics

There are **11 questions** in this test. Give yourself **10 minutes** to answer them all.

1. True or False? "Biofuels are made over millions of years from dead organic material."
   A True
   B False
   [1]

2. True or False? "Two isotopes of carbon will have the same number of neutrons but a different number of protons."
   A True
   B False
   [1]

3. What happens to the resistance of an LDR as the intensity of light shone on it increases?
   A It does not change
   B It increases
   C It decreases
   [1]

4. When a person jumps onto a trampoline, energy is transferred from the gravitational potential energy store of the person to the trampoline's elastic potential energy store...
   A ... electrically.
   B ... mechanically.
   C ... by heating.
   [1]

5. True or False? "A physical change is a type of chemical change."
   A True
   B False
   [1]

6. The radius of an atom is approximately...
   A ... 1×10^{-10} m.
   B ... 1×10^{-11} m.
   C ... 1×10^{-12} m.
   [1]

7. Electricity is transferred across step-up transformers to...
   A ... increase its potential difference for transmission from power stations.
   B ... increase its potential difference for domestic use.
   C ... increase its current for transmission from power stations.
   [1]

8. What happens in nuclear fusion?
   A One heavy nucleus emits a beta particle.
   B One heavy nucleus splits into two lighter nuclei.
   C Two light nuclei combine to form a heavier nucleus.
   [1]

Mixed Tests for Paper 1

9. What is the internal energy of a system?

....

....
[1]

10. An electric pencil sharpener has an efficiency of 75%. Calculate the amount of energy that is usefully transferred by the pencil sharpener if 560 J in total is supplied to it.

....

....

....

Energy = ... J
[3]

11. A sealed container with a moveable lid is filled with gas. The gas is compressed so that it has a volume of 290 cm³. The gas has a pressure of 160 kPa. The gas is then allowed to expand until its pressure reaches 110 kPa. If the temperature of the gas remains constant, calculate the new volume of the gas in cm³.

pressure × volume = constant

....

....

....

Volume = ... cm³
[3]

Test 14: Paper 1 Mixed Topics

There are **11 questions** in this test. Give yourself **10 minutes** to answer them all.

1. What colour of insulation is used to cover earth wires?

   A brown

   B blue

   C green and yellow stripes

   [1]

2. An apple with a mass of 0.1 kg hangs 2 m above the ground. Assuming the gravitational field strength is 9.8 N/kg, how much energy does the apple have in its gravitational potential energy store?

   A 0.49 J

   B 1.96 J

   C 4.90 J

   [1]

3. True or False? "A charged particle's electric field is weakest close to the charged particle."

   A True

   B False

   [1]

4. What happens to the temperature of an ice cube as it melts into water?

   A It stays the same

   B It increases

   C It decreases

   [1]

5. A current of 0.21 A flows through a resistor for 3 s. How much charge has passed through the resistor?

   A 0.07 C

   B 0.63 C

   C 1.89 C

   [1]

6. Which is the correct equation for density?

   A density = mass × volume

   B density = volume ÷ mass

   C density = mass ÷ volume

   [1]

7. What are the units of specific latent heat?

   A J/kg

   B J/°C

   C kg/J

   [1]

8. Which type of radiation is the most dangerous inside the body?

   A Alpha

   B Beta

   C Gamma

   [1]

9. A student uses a heater to supply 22 000 J of energy to a material with a mass of 540 g. The material has a specific heat capacity of 950 J/kg °C.
Calculate the temperature increase of the material.

   change in thermal energy = mass × specific heat capacity × temperature change

   ....

   ....

   ....

   Temperature increase = ... °C
   [3]

10. The equation below shows the alpha decay of an isotope of americium. Complete the equation by writing the missing atomic number and mass number of the product.

    $$^{241}_{95}\text{Am} \rightarrow {}^{\ldots}_{\ldots}\text{Np} + {}^{4}_{2}\text{He}$$

    [2]

11. An *I-V* graph for a circuit component is shown below.
    Identify the component and give a reason for your answer.

    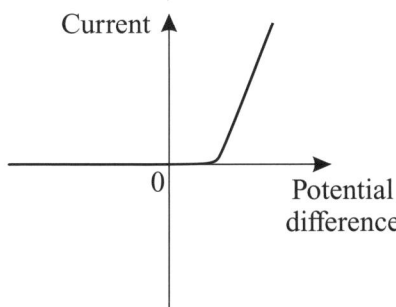

    Component: ....

    Reason: ....

    ....
    [2]

Test 15: Paper 1 Mixed Topics

There are **10 questions** in this test. Give yourself **10 minutes** to answer them all.

1. A speaker is connected to a 2 V battery. How much energy is transferred to the speaker when 80 C of charge passes through it?

   A   40 J

   B   82 J

   C   160 J
   [1]

2. True or False? "Some energy is always wasted when an electrical device is used."

   A   True

   B   False
   [1]

3. Why does increasing the volume in which a gas is contained at a constant temperature cause the pressure to decrease?

   A   The particles hit the walls of the container less often.

   B   The particles hit the walls of the container with less force.

   C   The particles hit the walls of the container at a slower speed.
   [1]

4. What is the activity of a radioactive source?

   A   The rate at which a source of unstable nuclei decays.

   B   The time taken for the number of nuclei of an isotope in a sample to halve.

   C   The amount of undecayed nuclei left in a sample at a given time.
   [1]

5. True or False? "Gamma rays are more strongly ionising than alpha particles."

   A   True

   B   False
   [1]

6. Which quantity is measured in pascals?

   A   Volume

   B   Charge

   C   Pressure
   [1]

7. Which of these is an environmental problem caused by generating electricity using hydro-electric power?

   A   It could result in a loss of habitat for some species.

   B   It results in the release of sulfur dioxide, which causes acid rain.

   C   The waste produced is dangerous and difficult to get rid of.
   [1]

8. Which of the following equations shows the correct relationship between the power of a device (P), its resistance (R) and the current flowing through it (I)?

   A $P = IR$

   B $P = I^2R$

   C $P = IR^2$
   [1]

9. A spring is extended by 34 mm, causing 0.45 J to be stored in its elastic potential energy store. Assuming the spring's limit of proportionality has not been reached, calculate the spring constant of the spring.

elastic potential energy = 0.5 × spring constant × (extension)^2

....

....

....

....

Spring constant = ... N/m

[3]

10. The cube below has a density of 8800 kg/m^3. Calculate the mass of the cube.

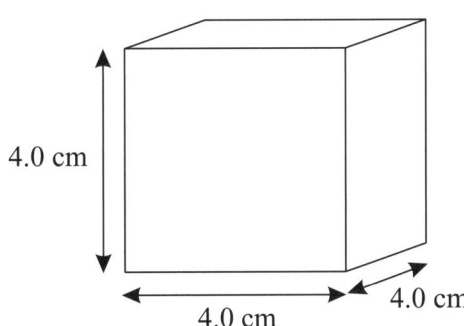

....

....

....

....

....

Mass = ... kg

[4]

Topics for Paper 2

Test 16: Forces

There are **10 questions** in this test. Give yourself **10 minutes** to answer them all.

1. How does the speed of a car affect its stopping distance at maximum braking force?

   A Higher speed results in a shorter stopping distance.

   B Higher speed results in a longer stopping distance.

   C The speed of the car doesn't matter.
   [1]

2. A teapot, weighing 10 N, is sat stationary on a table. What is the normal contact force applied to the teapot by the table?

   A 0 N

   B −10 N

   C −20 N
   [1]

3. Which of these is a typical running speed for a person?

   A 1 m/s

   B 3 m/s

   C 12 m/s
   [1]

4. How do seat belts reduce the risk of injury to wearers?

   A By slowing down the wearer more quickly.

   B By reducing the total change in momentum of the wearer.

   C By reducing the rate of change of momentum of the wearer.
   [1]

5. When a skydiver opens their parachute, their speed decreases because...

   A ... the air resistance acting on them increases.

   B ... the air resistance acting on them decreases.

   C ... their weight decreases.
   [1]

6. Brakes heat up when they're used because energy is transferred from...

   A ... the thermal energy stores of the brakes to the kinetic energy stores of the wheels.

   B ... the kinetic energy stores of the wheels to the thermal energy stores of the brakes.

   C ... the thermal energy stores of the wheels to the kinetic energy stores of the brakes.
   [1]

7. True or False? "If something's moving there must be an overall resultant force on it."

   A True

   B False
   [1]

8. The acceleration of an object is...

   A ... the change in height over time.

   B ... the change in position over time.

   C ... the change in velocity over time.
   [1]

Topics for Paper 2: Forces

9. Look at this graph.

   Describe the acceleration of the object between times A and D.

   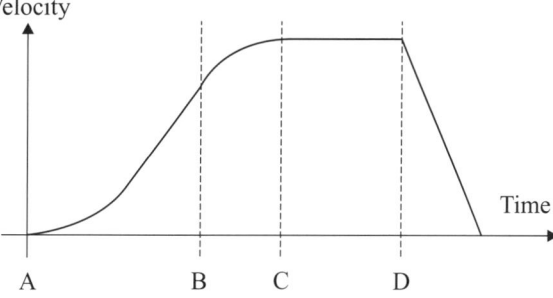

   ....

   ....

   ....

   ....

   ....
   [3]

10. The diagram below shows a gun being fired. The gun is initially stationary, then moves backwards when it is fired.

    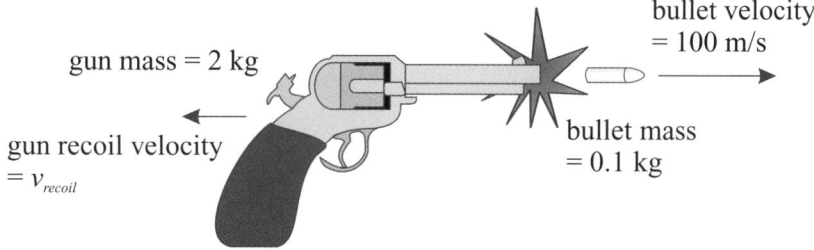

    Use the principle of conservation of momentum to find the recoil speed of the gun.

    ....

    ....

    ....

    ....

    Speed = ... m/s
    [4]

Test 17: Forces

There are **11 questions** in this test. Give yourself **10 minutes** to answer them all.

1. In a closed system, the total momentum after a collision is...

   A ... the same as the total momentum before the collision.

   B ... always zero.

   C ... greater than the total momentum before the collision.

   [1]

2. Up to the limit of proportionality, the extension of a stretched spring is...

   A ... directly proportional to the force applied.

   B ... inversely proportional to the force applied.

   C ... unrelated to the force applied.

   [1]

3. What is the correct equation to calculate the weight, W, of an object of mass m in a gravitational field of strength g?

   A $W = g \div m$

   B $W = m \times g$

   C $W = m \div g$

   [1]

4. What is the name of the point at which the weight of an object can be considered to act?

   A The centre of mass

   B The centre of weight

   C The centre of contact

   [1]

5. Which of these does not affect the braking distance of a car?

   A The car's speed

   B The condition of the car's tyres

   C The driver's reaction time

   [1]

6. If an object's momentum changes very quickly, the forces on the object will be...

   A ... large.

   B ... small.

   C ... unrelated to the rate of the momentum change.

   [1]

7. A force is applied to an object and causes an acceleration of 2.4 m/s². The same force is applied to a second object with half the mass of the first. What will the acceleration of the second object be?

   A 1.2 m/s²

   B 2.4 m/s²

   C 4.8 m/s²

   [1]

8. For a seesaw starting from rest, if the clockwise moments about it are equal to the anticlockwise moments about it, the seesaw will...

   A ... turn until its centre of mass is below the pivot.

   B ... start turning at a steady speed.

   C ... not turn.

   [1]

Topics for Paper 2: Forces

9. Explain how and why an object's speed changes as it falls through a fluid from rest to a terminal velocity.

   ....
   ....
   ....
   ....
   [3]

10. A pressure of 1.6 Pa acts on a hydraulic piston with an area of 2.5 m². Find the force applied by the hydraulic piston.

    ....
    ....
    ....

    Force = ... N
    [2]

11. Water has a density of 1000 kg/m³. An object is submerged in a tank of water 1.5 m below the surface. Calculate the pressure acting on the object due to the column of water above it. Assume the gravitational field strength is 9.8 N/kg.

    pressure due to a column of liquid = height of column × density of liquid
    × gravitational field strength

    ....
    ....
    ....

    Pressure = ... Pa
    [2]

Test 18: Forces

There are **11 questions** in this test. Give yourself **10 minutes** to answer them all.

1. A car accelerates from 9 m/s to 17 m/s in 4 s. What is the average acceleration of the car?

   A 2 m/s^2

   B 8 m/s^2

   C 32 m/s^2

   [1]

2. What is the typical speed of sound in air?

   A 330 m/s

   B 3×10^8 m/s

   C 3.3 m/s

   [1]

3. Which of the following correctly describes inertia?

   A The tendency for objects in motion to speed up.

   B The tendency for objects in motion to slow down.

   C The tendency for objects in motion to continue travelling at the same speed.

   [1]

4. Which of these is false?

   A When an object falls, work is done against gravity.

   B When an object falls, energy is lost from its gravitational potential energy store.

   C When an object is lifted, work is done against gravity.

   [1]

5. If the resultant force on a moving object is zero, the object will...

   A ... slow down and eventually stop.

   B ... keep moving at a steady speed.

   [1]

6. An object sinks in water if...

   A ... the upthrust on the object is more than the object's weight.

   B ... the upthrust on the object is less than the object's weight.

   C ... the upthrust on the object is equal to the object's weight.

   [1]

7. Simple levers are used...

   A ... to find the centre of mass of an object.

   B ... to find the number of forces acting on an object.

   C ... to transmit the rotational effects of forces.

   [1]

8. What unit is the joule equivalent to?

   A N/kg

   B N/m

   C Nm

   [1]

Topics for Paper 2: Forces

9. The graph on the right shows the motion of a cyclist.

   Use the graph to find the speed of the cyclist at 8 s.

   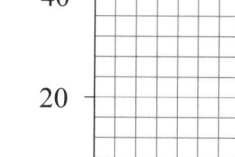

   ....

   ....

   ....

   Speed = ... m/s

   [2]

10. The object below is balanced on the pivot. Find the missing distance, x.

    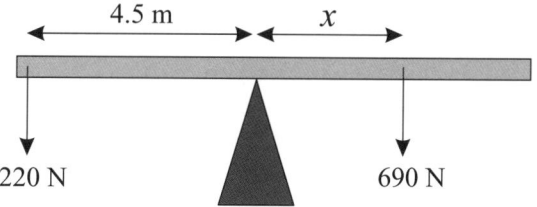

    ....

    ....

    ....

    $x = $ .... m

    [3]

11. Explain why the pressure of a fluid increases with depth.

    ....

    ....

    ....

    [2]

Test 19: Waves

There are **11 questions** in this test. Give yourself **10 minutes** to answer them all.

1. True or False? "Waves transfer matter."
   - A True
   - B False
   [1]

2. True or False? "The angle of incidence is equal to the angle of reflection."
   - A True
   - B False
   [1]

3. What units are used for wave speed?
   - A Metres, m.
   - B Metres per second, m/s.
   - C Hertz, Hz.
   [1]

4. Prolonged exposure to X-rays can kill body cells because they are...
   - A ... ionising.
   - B ... longitudinal waves.
   - C ...electromagnetic waves.
   [1]

5. What is the distance from the centre of a lens to the principal focus called?
   - A Convex length
   - B Focal length
   - C Principal length
   [1]

6. What is the 'normal' on a ray diagram?
   - A The length of a full cycle of a wave.
   - B A line drawn perpendicular to a surface at the point of incidence.
   - C The dull side of a mirror.
   [1]

7. Waves can change direction as they cross a boundary between two different substances. What is this called?
   - A Absorption
   - B Reflection
   - C Refraction
   [1]

8. Which of the following correctly describes 'radiation dose'?
   - A It is the total radiation that a person is exposed to.
   - B It is the probability of being exposed to radiation during an average day.
   - C It is a measure of the risk of harm to a person from exposure to radiation.
   [1]

Topics for Paper 2: Waves

9. Give one use of infrared radiation, and explain how it is suitable for this application.

   ....

   ....

   ....
   [2]

10. Describe what happens to the electrons in a radio receiver when it absorbs a radio wave.

    ....

    ....
    [1]

11. The ray diagram below shows light rays from an object meeting a convex lens. The object is placed exactly twice the focal length from the lens.

    Complete the ray diagram above to show the image formed by the lens. Describe the image type, and the size and orientation of the image.

    ....

    ....

    ....

    ....

    ....
    [4]

Test 20: Waves

There are **11 questions** in this test. Give yourself **10 minutes** to answer them all.

1. True or False? "All objects emit and absorb infrared radiation."

   A True
   B False
   [1]

2. What colour will a blue object appear when viewed through a red filter?

   A Blue
   B Red
   C Black
   [1]

3. True or False? "Radio waves are used for television broadcasts."

   A True
   B False
   [1]

4. True or False? "Waves are only refracted if they're travelling along the normal to the boundary they are crossing."

   A True
   B False
   [1]

5. Which of these is an example of a longitudinal wave?

   A Ripples on the surface of water
   B Sound waves
   C X-rays
   [1]

6. True or False? "A convex lens always produces a real image."

   A True
   B False
   [1]

7. Which of the following types of seismic waves can travel through liquids?

   A S-waves only
   B P-waves only
   C Both S-waves and P-waves
   [1]

8. Which of the following statements about electromagnetic (EM) waves is correct?

   A All EM waves travel through a vacuum at the same speed.
   B The higher the frequency of an EM wave, the faster it travels through a vacuum.
   C The higher the frequency of an EM wave, the slower it travels through a vacuum.
   [1]

Topics for Paper 2: Waves

9. Calculate the speed of a wave with a frequency of 3.0×10^7 Hz and a wavelength of 1.4 m.

....

....

....

Wave speed = ... m/s
[3]

10. Describe how ultrasound is used to produce images.

....

....

....

....

....
[3]

11. A light ray enters the block below at an angle to the normal. The block has a higher optical density than air. Sketch a light ray on the ray diagram below to show how the light ray may refract when it enters the block.

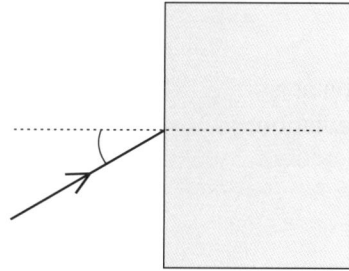

[1]

Test 21: Waves

There are **10 questions** in this test. Give yourself **10 minutes** to answer them all.

1. The different types of electromagnetic waves...

   A ... all have the same wavelength.

   B ... all have the same frequency.

   C ... form a continuous spectrum.

   [1]

2. In a longitudinal wave, the vibrations are...

   A ... parallel to the direction of energy transfer.

   B ... perpendicular to the direction of energy transfer.

   [1]

3. What is the range of human hearing?

   A 0 - 2000 Hz

   B 20 - 20 000 Hz

   C 2000 - 200 000 Hz

   [1]

4. Which of these is a use of gamma radiation?

   A Cooking food

   B Communications

   C Medical imaging

   [1]

5. Refraction is the process in which light...

   A ... bounces back as it hits a new medium.

   B ... changes direction as it enters a new medium.

   C ... transfers its energy to the medium as it enters that new medium.

   [1]

6. X-rays are suitable to be used in medical imaging because...

   A ... they are ionising.

   B ... some X-rays are always reflected at a boundary between different materials.

   C ... they are not transmitted by bones, but are transmitted by softer tissue.

   [1]

7. An object is absorbing infrared radiation at a faster rate than it is emitting infrared radiation. What is happening to its temperature?

   A It is decreasing

   B It remains constant

   C It is increasing

   [1]

8. What happens to the intensity of the radiation emitted by an object as its temperature increases?

   A It increases

   B It stays the same

   C It decreases

   [1]

Topics for Paper 2: Waves

9. On this oscilloscope trace of a wave, the timebase is set to 0.005 s/div.

   Calculate the frequency of the wave shown.

   $$\text{period} = \frac{1}{\text{frequency}}$$

   ....

   ....

   ....

   Frequency = ... Hz
   [3]

10. The diagram below shows the equipment used to form a wave on a string.

    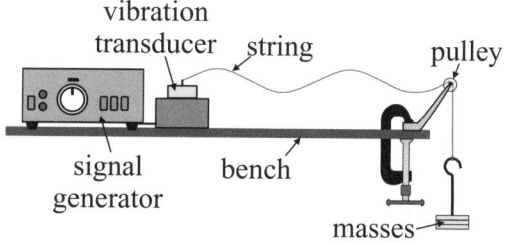

    Describe how you could accurately calculate the speed of the wave on the string.

    ....

    ....

    ....

    ....

    ....

    ....

    [4]

Test 22: Magnetism and Electromagnetism

There are **11 questions** in this test. Give yourself **10 minutes** to answer them all.

1. The force between the north poles of two bar magnets is...

   A ... attractive.

   B ... repulsive.

   [1]

2. Which of the following is a magnetic material?

   A Nickel

   B Silver

   C Copper

   [1]

3. The magnetic field produced when current flows through a wire...

   A ... is parallel to the wire.

   B ... is only at each end of the wire.

   C ... goes round the wire in circles centred on the wire.

   [1]

4. Which of these won't increase the rotational force acting on the rotating coil of wire in an electric motor?

   A Increasing the current.

   B Increasing the magnetic field strength.

   C Reversing the polarity of the magnets.

   [1]

5. True or False? "The magnetic field produced by a solenoid disappears when the current flowing through the solenoid is switched off."

   A True

   B False

   [1]

6. True or False? "A basic transformer is made up of a primary, secondary and tertiary coils, wrapped around an iron core."

   A True

   B False

   [1]

7. If an electrical conductor moves through a magnetic field...

   A ... the magnetic field disappears.

   B ... the magnetic field reverses.

   C ... a potential difference is induced in the conductor.

   [1]

8. True or False? "A step-up transformer is one where the potential difference across the primary coil is higher than the potential difference across the secondary coil."

   A True

   B False

   [1]

Topics for Paper 2: Magnetism and Electromagnetism

9. In which direction will this coil turn, clockwise or anticlockwise?

....
[1]

10. A current-carrying wire is placed between the north and south poles of two bar magnets at 90° to the magnetic field between the poles. The magnets exert a force of 176 μN on the wire. The length of wire within the magnetic field of the bar magnets is 1.1 cm. The current flowing through the wire is 0.80 A.
What is the magnetic field strength of the magnetic field caused by the two bar magnets?

force = magnetic field strength × current × length

....

....

....

....

Magnetic field strength = ... T
[3]

11. How can a rotating magnet be used to generate an alternating current in a coil of wire?

....

....

....

....
[3]

Test 23: Magnetism and Electromagnetism

There are **11 questions** in this test. Give yourself **10 minutes** to answer them all.

1. True or False? "The magnetic field of a bar magnet is strongest at the poles."
   A True
   B False
   [1]

2. True or False? "Loudspeakers work using the generator effect."
   A True
   B False
   [1]

3. A plotting compass can be used to get information about...
   A ... the strength of a magnetic field only.
   B ... the direction of a magnetic field only.
   C ... the strength and direction of a magnetic field.
   [1]

4. A motor consists of a spinning coil of wire in a magnetic field. To keep the coil spinning, you need to...
   A ... increase the current every half turn.
   B ... increase the magnetic field strength every half turn.
   C ... swap the contacts every half turn.
   [1]

5. True or False? "A changing magnetic field around the iron core of a transformer induces an alternating potential difference across the secondary coil."
   A True
   B False
   [1]

6. A lump of unmagnetised iron becomes an induced magnet when placed next to a bar magnet. When the bar magnet is removed, the magnetic field strength of the iron...
   A ... decreases.
   B ... increases.
   C ... stays the same.
   [1]

7. An iron core can be placed in the middle of a current-carrying solenoid to...
   A ... change the shape of the magnetic field of the solenoid.
   B ... increase the strength of the magnetic field of the solenoid.
   C ... change the direction of the magnetic field of the solenoid.
   [1]

8. Which of these correctly describes a dynamo?
   A Dynamos are generators that use slip rings and brushes to produce an alternating current.
   B Dynamos are generators that use a split-ring commutator to produce a direct current.
   C Dynamos are generators that use slip rings and brushes to produce a direct current.
   [1]

Topics for Paper 2: Magnetism and Electromagnetism

9. The diagram shows the force on a current-carrying wire in a magnetic field.

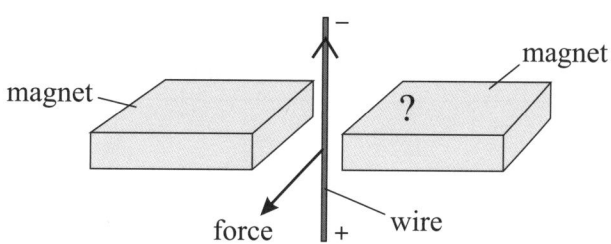

Does the '?' in the diagram mark the north (N) or south (S) pole of the magnet? ....
Justify your answer.

....

....
[2]

10. State the approximate direction in which a compass will point if it is not near to any magnetised materials, and explain why the compass points in this direction.

....

....

....
[2]

11. The potential difference across a transformer increases from 230 V on the primary coil to 400 000 V on the secondary coil. If the current in the secondary coil is 0.018 A, what is the current in the primary coil?

        potential difference across primary coil × current in primary coil
        = potential difference across secondary coil × current in secondary coil

....

....

....

....

Current = ... A
[3]

Test 24: Space Physics

There are **11 questions** in this test. Give yourself **10 minutes** to answer them all.

1. What name is given to the observed increase in the wavelength of light coming from distant galaxies?

   A The Big Bang theory
   B Expansion theory
   C Red-shift
   [1]

2. Which process releases energy in stars?

   A Combustion
   B Nuclear fission
   C Nuclear fusion
   [1]

3. A star much bigger than the Sun is in the 'main sequence' stage of its life. What is the next stage in its life cycle?

   A A red giant
   B A red super giant
   C A supernova
   [1]

4. True or False? "All the elements found on Earth were formed during the stable period of a star's life."

   A True
   B False
   [1]

5. Scientists currently believe that when the universe began it was...

   A ... small, dense and hot.
   B ... identical to the current universe.
   C ... much larger and cooler than the current universe.
   [1]

6. True or False? "If the speed of a planet orbiting a star changes, then the radius of its orbit must also change for it to remain in a stable orbit."

   A True
   B False
   [1]

7. In general, the further away a galaxy is...

   A ... the smaller the observed increase in the wavelength of its light.
   B ... the slower it is moving away from us.
   C ... the bigger the observed increase in wavelength of its light.
   [1]

8. How many planets are there in our solar system?

   A 8
   B 9
   C 10
   [1]

Topics for Paper 2: Space Physics

9. Explain why stars stay stable in their main sequence phase.

   ....

   ....

   ....
   [2]

10. Explain why the velocity of a planet undergoing circular motion changes but its speed does not.

    ....

    ....

    ....

    ....
    [2]

11. The diagram below shows some of the solar system. Complete the labels.

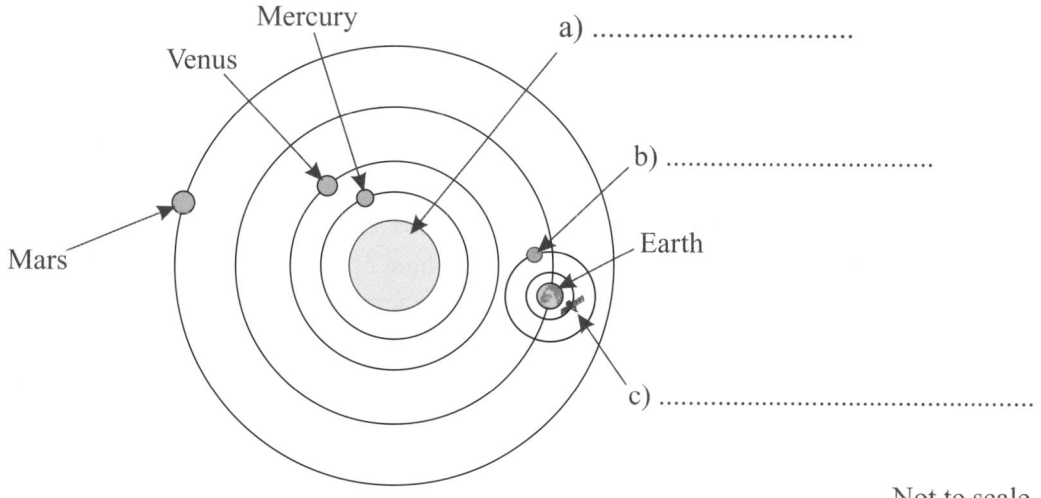

Not to scale

[3]

Test 25: Space Physics

There are **10 questions** in this test. Give yourself **10 minutes** to answer them all.

1. True or False? "The life cycle of a star depends on its size."

   A True
   B False
   [1]

2. Which of the following orbit the Sun?

   A Stars
   B Galaxies
   C Dwarf planets
   [1]

3. What is a moon?

   A A natural satellite that orbits a planet.
   B An artificial satellite that orbits a planet.
   C A natural satellite that orbits a star.
   [1]

4. True or False? "Earth is located in the Milky Way galaxy."

   A True
   B False
   [1]

5. True or False? "Elements with a higher mass than helium are only formed in supernovae."

   A True
   B False
   [1]

6. In general, galaxies at a greater distance from Earth are moving away...

   A ... faster than nearer ones.
   B ... slower than nearer ones.
   C ... at the same speed as nearer ones.
   [1]

7. What force allows planets and satellites to maintain their circular orbits?

   A Magnetic
   B Electrostatic
   C Gravity
   [1]

8. Which of the following is not formed after a supernova?

   A A neutron star
   B A black hole
   C A red super giant
   [1]

Topics for Paper 2: Space Physics

9. Fill in the labels below to complete the life cycle of the star.

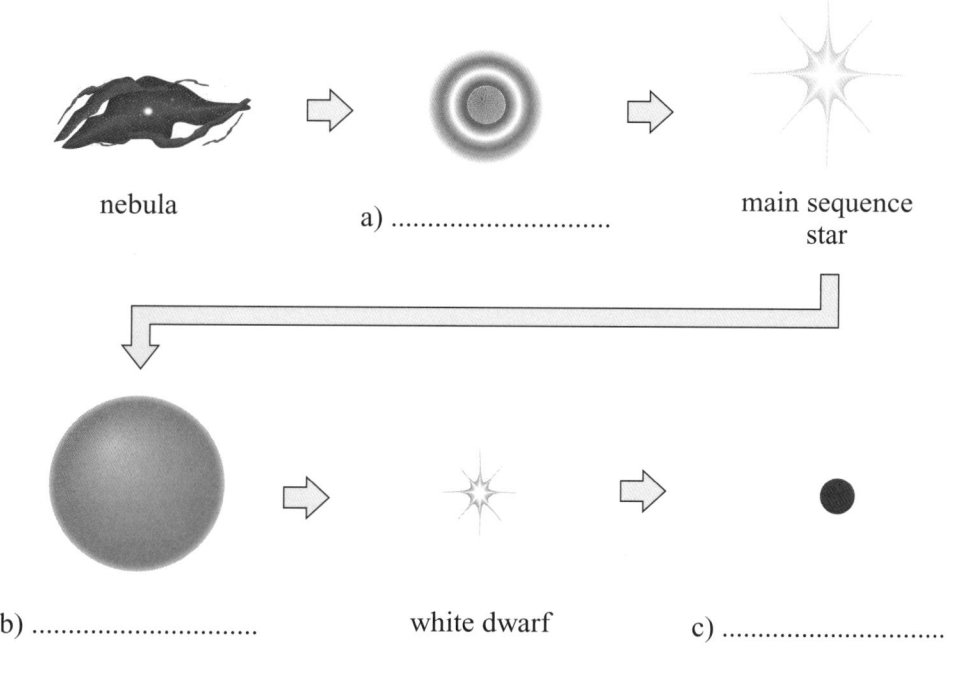

nebula a) .... main sequence star

b) .... white dwarf c) ....

[3]

10. Explain how red-shift provides evidence for the Big Bang theory.

....

....

....

....

....

....

[4]

Test 26: Paper 2 Mixed Topics

There are **11 questions** in this test. Give yourself **10 minutes** to answer them all.

1. True or False? "If an object's slowing down, there must be a non-zero resultant force acting on it."

   A   True

   B   False

   [1]

2. Car safety features are designed to...

   A   ... decrease the time taken for a passenger's momentum to change.

   B   ... increase the time taken for a passenger's momentum to change.

   [1]

3. When a planet orbits a star it continuously accelerates due to a force acting...

   A   ... away from the centre of the star.

   B   ... in the direction it's travelling in.

   C   ... towards the centre of the star.

   [1]

4. A current-carrying wire in a magnetic field won't feel a force if it's...

   A   ... parallel to the magnetic field.

   B   ... at 45° to the magnetic field.

   C   ... perpendicular to the magnetic field.

   [1]

5. The point at which all of an object's mass may be thought to be concentrated is called the...

   A   ... centre of mass.

   B   ... moment.

   C   ... pivot.

   [1]

6. An object submerged in a fluid experiences upthrust because the fluid pressure at the bottom of the object is...

   A   ... smaller than the fluid pressure at the top of the object.

   B   ... equal to the fluid pressure at the top of the object.

   C   ... larger than the fluid pressure at the top of the object.

   [1]

7. What is a nebula?

   A   A dense point in space from which light cannot escape.

   B   An explosion that occurs at the end of a large star's life.

   C   A cloud of dust and gas from which stars are formed.

   [1]

8. An electromagnetic wave slows down as it enters a different medium at an angle to the normal. What happens to the wave's direction?

   A   It bends away from the normal.

   B   It bends towards the normal.

   C   It continues travelling at the same angle to the normal.

   [1]

9. A bar magnet is shown below. Draw the magnetic field pattern of the bar magnet on the diagram, including arrows to show the direction of the field.

N   S

[2]

10. A pulse of ultrasound is emitted towards a boundary, where it is reflected back to the source. It is detected at the source 1×10^{-5} s after it is emitted. If the speed of ultrasound is 2000 m/s, how far away is the boundary?

....

....

....

Distance = ... m

[3]

11. Describe one use of microwaves in communications and explain why microwaves are suitable for this purpose.

....

....

....

....

[2]

Test 27: Paper 2 Mixed Topics

There are **11 questions** in this test. Give yourself **10 minutes** to answer them all.

1. An opaque black object...
   A ... reflects all wavelengths of visible light.
   B ... transmits all wavelengths of visible light.
   C ... absorbs all wavelengths of visible light.
   [1]

2. True or False? "S-waves are longitudinal waves and P-waves are transverse waves."
   A True
   B False
   [1]

3. What is the frequency of a wave?
   A The number of waves passing a point per second.
   B The distance travelled by the wave each second.
   C The distance from one crest on a wave to the next adjacent crest.
   [1]

4. In Fleming's left-hand rule, the directions of which variables are represented by your thumb and first two fingers?
   A Force, current and magnetic field
   B Current and magnetic field only
   C Force, magnetic field and induced potential difference
   [1]

5. Which of these is a typical value for a person's reaction time?
   A 0.04 s
   B 0.4 s
   C 4 s
   [1]

6. To travel at a constant speed, the driving force of a car engine must...
   A ... be less than the frictional forces.
   B ... balance the frictional forces.
   C ... exceed the frictional forces.
   [1]

7. True or False? "If nickel is put in a magnetic field, it will become an induced magnet."
   A True
   B False
   [1]

8. Which of the following is a contact force?
   A Gravitational force
   B Electrostatic force
   C Air resistance
   [1]

9. A student suspends a spring from a clamp and hangs different weights from it. She plots the force exerted by each weight against the extension of the spring that it produces on the graph on the right. What is the gradient of this graph equal to?

    ....
    [1]

10. Explain how a main sequence star is formed from a protostar.

    ....

    ....

    ....

    ....
    [2]

11. The diagram on the right shows a Leslie cube. A Leslie cube is a hollow metal cube that can be filled with water. It has four vertical faces. Each face is made from the same material, but they have different colours and surfaces. Describe a method that can be used to compare the amount of radiation emitted from its matt black face to the amount emitted from its shiny white face.

    ....

    ....

    ....

    ....

    ....

    ....
    [4]

Test 28: Paper 2 Mixed Topics

There are **10 questions** in this test. Give yourself **10 minutes** to answer them all.

1. X-rays are...

   A ... electromagnetic waves.

   B ... sound waves.

   C ... radio waves.

   [1]

2. Which type of lens can only form virtual images?

   A Convex lens

   B Concave lens

   [1]

3. An object that does not transmit any light is described as...

   A ... translucent.

   B ... transparent.

   C ... opaque.

   [1]

4. Loudspeakers convert...

   A ... pressure variations into variations in current.

   B ... variations in current into pressure variations.

   C ... variations in current into electromagnetic waves.

   [1]

5. True or False? "A black hole is always produced after a supernova."

   A True

   B False

   [1]

6. Which of these is a typical walking speed?

   A 1.5 m/s

   B 4.5 m/s

   C 12 m/s

   [1]

7. What do observations of supernovae since 1998 suggest?

   A That the rate at which distant galaxies are receding from us isn't changing.

   B That the rate at which distant galaxies are receding from us is decreasing.

   C That the rate at which distant galaxies are receding from us is increasing.

   [1]

8. Which of the following does not affect the size of the force on a conductor in a magnetic field at 90° to the field?

   A The size of the current through the conductor

   B The length of the conductor inside the magnetic field

   C The direction of the current

   [1]

9. Explain how an alternating current in the primary coil of a transformer creates an alternating potential difference across the secondary coil.

....

....

....

....

....
[3]

10. An 8 m rod weighing 1500 N is suspended horizontally at rest. The rod is attached to a pivot at one end, and supported by a vertical rope at the other, as shown in the diagram.

If the weight of the rod acts at its centre, find the upwards force applied to the rod by the rope.

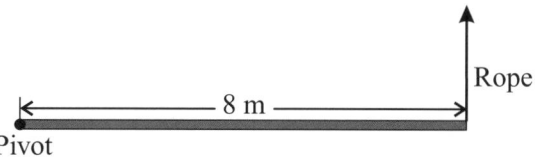

....

....

....

....

Force = ... N
[4]

Test 29: Paper 2 Mixed Topics

There are **11 questions** in this test. Give yourself **10 minutes** to answer them all.

1. Which of these will cause a change in the direction of the force acting on a conductor at 90° to a magnetic field?

    A Reversing the current through the conductor.

    B Increasing the length of the conductor.

    C Reducing the magnetic flux density of the magnetic field.

    [1]

2. In a step-up transformer, the secondary coil has...

    A ... fewer turns than the primary coil.

    B ... the same number of turns as the primary coil.

    C ... more turns than the primary coil.

    [1]

3. A skydiver has a weight of 750 N. The drag acting upwards on the skydiver is 600 N. What is the resultant vertical force acting on the skydiver?

    A 150 N upwards

    B 150 N downwards

    C 750 N downwards

    [1]

4. Object A is travelling to the left and collides with the stationary object B. After the collision, object B moves away to the left. Which of the following is true of object A's momentum after the collision?

    A It is the same as it was before the collision.

    B It is lower than it was before the collision.

    C It is higher than it was before the collision.

    [1]

5. Two toy cars with the same mass are pushed with different forces. The car pushed with a greater force has...

    A ... a greater acceleration than the other car.

    B ... a lower acceleration than the other car.

    C ... the same acceleration as the other car.

    [1]

6. Roughly how far would a sound wave travel through the air in 3 s?

    A 110 m

    B 330 m

    C 990 m

    [1]

7. Which of the following will our Sun eventually become?

    A A neutron star

    B A black hole

    C A black dwarf

    [1]

8. As the height above the Earth's surface increases...

    A ... atmospheric pressure increases.

    B ... atmospheric pressure decreases.

    C ... atmospheric pressure stays the same.

    [1]

Mixed Tests for Paper 2

9. A lens provides a magnification of 3.
   If it forms an image 13.5 cm high, how tall is the object?

   magnification = image height ÷ object height

   ....

   ....

   Height = ... cm
   [2]

10. A student is investigating how light reflects from different surfaces. He shines a ray of light onto a sheet of rough card and then onto a plane mirror, using the same angle of incidence each time. Compare how the light will reflect differently from the card and from the mirror.

    ....

    ....

    ....

    ....
    [2]

11. A velocity-time graph for a racing car is shown on the right.

    Calculate the distance travelled by the car in the first 15 s of its journey.

    ....

    ....

    ....

    Distance = ... m
    [3]

Test 30: Paper 2 Mixed Topics

There are **10 questions** in this test. Give yourself **10 minutes** to answer them all.

1. How much force would be needed to accelerate a 6 kg object by 3 m/s²?

   A   0.5 N
   B   2 N
   C   18 N

   [1]

2. The magnetic field inside a solenoid is...

   A   ... weak and uniform.
   B   ... strong and uniform.
   C   ... strong and irregular.

   [1]

3. What would happen to the Earth's temperature if the atmosphere began absorbing more radiation than it emitted?

   A   It would increase.
   B   It would decrease.

   [1]

4. True or False? "Red-shift provides evidence that the universe is contracting."

   A   True
   B   False

   [1]

5. How much force is needed to elastically stretch a spring with a spring constant of 30 N/m by 0.03 m?

   A   0.001 N
   B   0.027 N
   C   0.9 N

   [1]

6. The amplitude of a wave is...

   A   ... the distance between the same point on two adjacent waves.
   B   ... the number of waves passing a point per second.
   C   ... the maximum displacement of a point on a wave from its undisturbed position.

   [1]

7. The direction of the arrows on a magnetic field line at a point is given by the direction of the force that would act on...

   A   ... a north pole placed at that point.
   B   ... a south pole placed at that point.
   C   ... a magnetic material placed at that point.

   [1]

8. Which of the following equations correctly shows the relationship between the momentum, p, mass, m, and velocity, v, of a body?

   A $p = mv$
   B $p = m \div v$
   C $p = v \div m$

   [1]

Mixed Tests for Paper 2

9. A student sets up water waves with a frequency of 4.0 Hz in a ripple tank. She measures the distance shown in the diagram to be 42 cm.

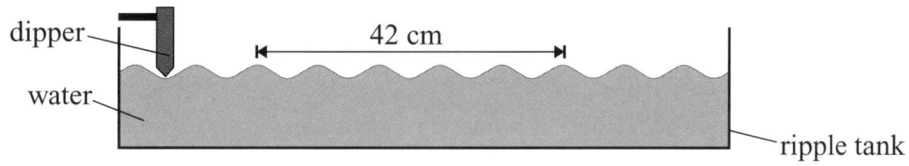

Calculate the speed of the waves.

....

....

....

Wave speed = ... m/s

[3]

10. A boat has a driving force of 800 N east. The wind produces a force on the boat of 350 N north. Draw a scale diagram to find the magnitude and direction of the resultant force on the boat. Give your direction as an angle, clockwise from north.

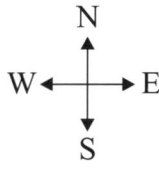

Magnitude = ... N

Direction = ... ° clockwise from north

[4]

15

Answers

Topics for Paper 1

Test 1: Energy
Pages 2–3
1. A *[1 mark]*
2. C *[1 mark]*
3. B *[1 mark]*
4. A *[1 mark]*
5. B *[1 mark]*
6. B *[1 mark]*
7. A *[1 mark]*
8. A *[1 mark]*
9. $E_k = \frac{1}{2}mv^2$
   $= \frac{1}{2} \times 160 \times 8.5^2$ *[1 mark]*
   $= 5780$ J *[1 mark]*
10. Any two from: e.g. Radioactive waste is produced, which is difficult to dispose of safely. / It's expensive to set up and close down nuclear power stations. / There is a risk of radiation leaks and catastrophes. *[2 marks]*
11. 500 g = 0.5 kg
    Specific heat capacity = energy / (mass × temperature change) *[1 mark]*
    Specific heat capacity
    $= 2925 / (0.5 \times 15)$ *[1 mark]*
    $= 390$ J/kg°C *[1 mark]*

Test 2: Energy
Pages 4–5
1. C *[1 mark]*
2. A *[1 mark]*
3. A *[1 mark]*
4. B *[1 mark]*
5. A *[1 mark]*
6. C *[1 mark]*
7. B *[1 mark]*
8. C *[1 mark]*
9. E.g. They can alter the landscape/spoil the view. They can alter the local habitat for wildlife. *[2 marks]*
10. Block C *[1 mark]*, as it has the lowest temperature change for the given amount of energy supplied *[1 mark]*.
11. 2 mins = 2 × 60 = 120 s *[1 mark]*
    power = energy transferred
                ÷ time taken
    Rearrange the formula:
    energy transferred
        = power × time taken
        = 50 × 120 *[1 mark]*
        = 6000 J *[1 mark]*
    [Or 3 marks for the correct answer via any other method.]

Test 3: Energy
Pages 6–7
1. A *[1 mark]*
2. A *[1 mark]*
3. B *[1 mark]*
4. C *[1 mark]*
5. C *[1 mark]*
6. B *[1 mark]*
7. B *[1 mark]*
8. B *[1 mark]*
9. A hairdryer transfers energy electrically from the mains to the thermal energy store of the hairdryer heater *[1 mark]* and the kinetic energy store of the fan blades *[1 mark]*.

10. 500 g = 0.5 kg
    Rearrange the formula:
    change in height = change in gravitational potential energy ÷ (mass × g) *[1 mark]*
    $= 100 \div (0.5 \times 9.8)$ *[1 mark]*
    $= 20.40...$
    $= 20$ m (to 2 s.f.) *[1 mark]*
11. A is the best insulator *[1 mark]* as the flask decreases in temperature by the smallest amount *[1 mark]*.

Test 4: Electricity
Pages 8–9
1. B *[1 mark]*
2. B *[1 mark]*
3. C *[1 mark]*
4. B *[1 mark]*
5. A *[1 mark]*
6. A *[1 mark]*
7. C *[1 mark]*
8. B *[1 mark]*
9. Resistance is directly proportional to the length of the conductor *[1 mark]*.
10. Convert energy into J:
    5.4 kJ = 5400 J *[1 mark]*
    energy = charge × potential difference / $E = QV$
    Rearrange the formula:
    $Q = E \div V$
    $= 5400 \div 1.2$ *[1 mark]*
    $= 4500$ C *[1 mark]*
11. As more current flows through the lamp, the temperature of the filament increases *[1 mark]*. As the temperature increases, the resistance increases *[1 mark]*. The greater the resistance, the flatter the graph, so the graph curves as the current increases *[1 mark]*.

Test 5: Electricity
Pages 10–11
1. A *[1 mark]*
2. B *[1 mark]*
3. A *[1 mark]*
4. A *[1 mark]*
5. A *[1 mark]*
6. C *[1 mark]*
7. C *[1 mark]*
8. C *[1 mark]*
9. In a series circuit, the supply potential difference is shared, so:
   $V_3 = V_1 + V_2 = 3 + 2 = 5$ V *[1 mark]*
   Resistances add up, so:
   $R = R_1 + R_2 = 6 + 4 = 10$ Ω *[1 mark]*
   The ammeter will measure the total current. The current can be calculated using the supply potential difference and the total resistance of the circuit. (Alternatively, it could be calculated using the potential difference across R_1 or R_2.)
   potential difference = current × resistance / $V = IR$

   Rearrange the formula:
   $I = V \div R$
   $= V_3 \div R$
   $= 5 \div 10$ *[1 mark]*
   $= 0.5$ A *[1 mark]*
10. Transformers *[1 mark]*. Transformers are used to increase the potential difference and decrease the current of electricity for energy-efficient transmission *[1 mark]*. They are then used to reduce the potential difference to a safe, usable level when it reaches consumers *[1 mark]*.

Test 6: Electricity
Pages 12–13
1. B *[1 mark]*
2. A *[1 mark]*
3. A *[1 mark]*
4. C *[1 mark]*
5. B *[1 mark]*
6. C *[1 mark]*
7. C *[1 mark]*
8. A *[1 mark]*
9. *[1 mark for straight field lines at 90° to surface of sphere, 1 mark for field lines pointing towards the sphere]*
10. When the materials are rubbed together, negatively charged electrons are rubbed off one material and move onto the other *[1 mark]*. This leaves the material they've moved off with a positive charge, and the material they've moved onto with an equal negative charge *[1 mark]*.
11. Power = potential difference
           × current / $P = VI$
    Rearrange the formula:
    $I = P \div V$ *[1 mark]*
    $= 150 \div 230$ *[1 mark]*
    $= 0.652...$
    $= 0.65$ A (to 2 s.f.) *[1 mark]*

Test 7: Particle Model of Matter
Pages 14–15
1. B *[1 mark]*
2. B *[1 mark]*
3. A *[1 mark]*
4. C *[1 mark]*
5. C *[1 mark]*
6. B *[1 mark]*
7. C *[1 mark]*
8. B *[1 mark]*
9. Particles in a solid are held close together in a regular arrangement, whereas particles in a gas are far apart and are free to move *[1 mark]*.

Answers

10. 855 kJ/kg = 855 000 J/kg *[1 mark]*
    thermal energy for a change of state
    = mass × specific latent heat
    = 0.60 × 855 000 *[1 mark]*
    = 513 000 J *[1 mark]*
11. The gas applies pressure to the plunger of the pump/outside of the tyre, and so exerts a force on it *[1 mark]*. Work has to be done against this force to push down the plunger on the pump/push more gas into the tyre *[1 mark]*. This transfers energy to the kinetic energy stores of the gas particles, increasing the temperature *[1 mark]*.

Test 8: Particle Model of Matter
Pages 16–17

1. B *[1 mark]*   2. A *[1 mark]*
3. A *[1 mark]*   4. C *[1 mark]*
5. C *[1 mark]*   6. A *[1 mark]*
7. A *[1 mark]*   8. B *[1 mark]*
9. solid *[1 mark]*
10. density = mass ÷ volume
    = 0.386 ÷ (2.00 × 10^{-5}) *[1 mark]*
    = 19 300 kg/m^3 *[1 mark]*
11. Fill the eureka can with water to just below the spout, and place a measuring cylinder beneath the spout *[1 mark]*. Submerge the object in the water and collect the displaced water in the measuring cylinder *[1 mark]*. Record the volume of water in the measuring cylinder, which is equal to the volume of the object *[1 mark]*. Substitute the object's mass and volume into density = mass ÷ volume to find its density *[1 mark]*.

Test 9: Atomic Structure
Pages 18–19

1. A *[1 mark]*   2. C *[1 mark]*
3. B *[1 mark]*   4. C *[1 mark]*
5. B *[1 mark]*   6. A *[1 mark]*
7. A *[1 mark]*   8. B *[1 mark]*
9. An atom is electrically neutral, but an ion is charged. / An atom has the same number of protons and electrons, but an ion doesn't *[1 mark]*.
10. $^{32}_{16}$S
    [1 mark for each correct number]
11. Half-life = 4 hours
    [2 marks for a correct answer, otherwise 1 mark for an attempt to find the half-life using a correct method.]

12. Irradiation is when an object is exposed to radiation emitted by a radioactive source *[1 mark]* while contamination is when (unwanted) atoms of a radioactive source get on/inside another object *[1 mark]*.

Test 10: Atomic Structure
Pages 20–21

1. B *[1 mark]*   2. A *[1 mark]*
3. A *[1 mark]*   4. C *[1 mark]*
5. A *[1 mark]*   6. A *[1 mark]*
7. B *[1 mark]*   8. B *[1 mark]*
9. Keep halving the initial count rate until it is at the level required:
   960 ÷ 2 = 480
   480 ÷ 2 = 240
   240 ÷ 2 = 120
   Count how many times you had to halve it (3), and multiply this number by the half-life of the sample:
   3 × 30 = 90 minutes
   [2 marks for the correct answer, otherwise 1 mark for any correct method.]
10. When an electron in an atom absorbs an electromagnetic wave, the electron moves to a higher energy level *[1 mark]*, and it will orbit further from the nucleus *[1 mark]*.
11. When a nuclear fission reaction occurs, a number of neutrons are emitted *[1 mark]*. These neutrons can be absorbed by other nuclei *[1 mark]* and trigger other nuclear fission reactions that also release neutrons, causing a chain reaction *[1 mark]*.

Mixed Tests for Paper 1
Test 11: Paper 1 Mixed Topics
Pages 22–23

1. B *[1 mark]*   2. A *[1 mark]*
3. A *[1 mark]*   4. B *[1 mark]*
5. A *[1 mark]*   6. B *[1 mark]*
7. A *[1 mark]*   8. C *[1 mark]*
9. Ionising radiation can kill cells *[1 mark]*. It can be targeted at a tumour to kill cancer cells and control its growth *[1 mark]*
10. In a parallel circuit, each component is connected separately to the power supply *[1 mark]*. When one bulb blows, only that part of the circuit is broken — current can still flow through the part connecting the other bulb to the power supply, so the light stays on *[1 mark]*.

11. There are initially 14 000 radioactive nuclei, so after one half-life there will be 7000 radioactive nuclei.
    Reading from graph:
    half-life = 5.6 × 10^3 years *[1 mark]*
    16.8 × 10^3 years is
    (16.8 × 10^3) ÷ (5.6 × 10^3)
    = 3 half-lives
    Number of radioactive nuclei left after 2 half-lives
    = 7000 ÷ 2 = 3500 *[1 mark]*
    Number of radioactive nuclei left after 3 half-lives
    = 3500 ÷ 2 = 1750 *[1 mark]*

Test 12: Paper 1 Mixed Topics
Pages 24–25

1. A *[1 mark]*   2. A *[1 mark]*
3. C *[1 mark]*   4. B *[1 mark]*
5. C *[1 mark]*   6. A *[1 mark]*
7. A *[1 mark]*   8. B *[1 mark]*
9. E.g. If the count-rate reduces significantly when the paper is used, then the source emits alpha radiation *[1 mark]*. If the count rate is greatly reduced by the aluminium but not the paper, then the source emits beta radiation *[1 mark]*. If the count rate isn't greatly reduced by either sheet then the source emits gamma radiation *[1 mark]*.
10. Thermistor *[1 mark]*
    Total circuit resistance
    = 2.0 + 3.0 = 5.0 Ω *[1 mark]*
    Rearrange $V = IR$ for I:
    $I = V \div R$ = 9.3 ÷ 5.0 *[1 mark]*
    = 1.86 A
    = 1.9 A (to 2 s.f.) *[1 mark]*

Test 13: Paper 1 Mixed Topics
Pages 26–27

1. B *[1 mark]*   2. B *[1 mark]*
3. C *[1 mark]*   4. B *[1 mark]*
5. B *[1 mark]*   6. A *[1 mark]*
7. A *[1 mark]*   8. C *[1 mark]*
9. The energy stored inside a system by the particles that make up the system / the total kinetic energy and potential energy of all the particles that make up a system *[1 mark]*
10. 75% = 0.75
    efficiency = useful output energy transfer ÷ total input energy transfer
    Rearrange the equation:
    useful output energy transfer = efficiency × total input energy transfer *[1 mark]*
    = 0.75 × 560 *[1 mark]*
    = 420 J *[1 mark]*

Answers

11. pressure (p) × volume (V) = constant so $p_1V_1 = p_2V_2$ *[1 mark]*
    Rearrange for V_2:
    $$V_2 = \frac{p_1 V_1}{p_2}$$
    Since this is a ratio, you don't need to change the units into Pa and m³.
    $$V_2 = \frac{160 \times 290}{110}$$ *[1 mark]*
    = 421.8... cm³
    = 420 cm³ (to 2 s.f.) *[1 mark]*

Test 14: Paper 1 Mixed Topics
Pages 28–29
1. C *[1 mark]*   2. B *[1 mark]*
3. B *[1 mark]*   4. A *[1 mark]*
5. B *[1 mark]*   6. C *[1 mark]*
7. A *[1 mark]*   8. A *[1 mark]*
9. 540 g = 0.54 kg
   $\Delta E = mc\Delta\theta$
   Rearrange for $\Delta\theta$:
   $$\Delta\theta = \frac{\Delta E}{mc}$$ *[1 mark]*
   $$= \frac{22\,000}{0.54 \times 950}$$ *[1 mark]*
   = 42.88...
   = 43 °C (to 2 s.f.) *[1 mark]*
10. $^{241}_{95}\text{Am} \rightarrow {}^{237}_{93}\text{Np} + {}^{4}_{2}\text{He}$
    [1 mark for correct mass number and 1 mark for correct atomic number.]
11. Diode *[1 mark]*. The I-V graph shows that current only flows in one direction / there is a very high resistance in the reverse direction *[1 mark]*.

Test 15: Paper 1 Mixed Topics
Pages 30–31
1. C *[1 mark]*   2. A *[1 mark]*
3. A *[1 mark]*   4. A *[1 mark]*
5. B *[1 mark]*   6. C *[1 mark]*
7. A *[1 mark]*   8. B *[1 mark]*
9. 34 mm = 0.034 m *[1 mark]*
   elastic potential energy = 0.5 × spring constant × (extension)²
   or $E_e = \frac{1}{2}ke^2$
   Rearrange for k:
   $$k = \frac{2E_e}{e^2} = \frac{2 \times 0.45}{0.034^2}$$ *[1 mark]*
   = 778.5... N/m
   = 780 N/m (to 2 s.f.) *[1 mark]*
10. 4.0 cm = 0.040 m
    So the volume of the cube is
    0.040 × 0.040 × 0.040
    = 6.4 × 10⁻⁵ m³ *[1 mark]*
    density = mass ÷ volume

Rearrange for mass:
mass = density × volume *[1 mark]*
     = 8800 × 6.4 × 10⁻⁵ *[1 mark]*
     = 0.5632 kg
     = 0.56 kg (to 2 s.f.) *[1 mark]*

Topics for Paper 2

Test 16: Forces
Pages 32–33
1. B *[1 mark]*   2. B *[1 mark]*
3. B *[1 mark]*   4. C *[1 mark]*
5. A *[1 mark]*   6. B *[1 mark]*
7. B *[1 mark]*   8. C *[1 mark]*
9. Between A and B, the acceleration of the object increases at an increasing rate for approximately half the time, then the object has a constant acceleration *[1 mark]*. Between B and C the object's acceleration gradually decreases *[1 mark]*. Between C and D the object travels at a steady velocity / has an acceleration of 0 m/s² *[1 mark]*.
10. total momentum before collision = total momentum after collision *[1 mark]*
    Bullet momentum
    = mass × velocity
    = 0.1 × 100 = 10 kg m/s *[1 mark]*
    So gun's momentum is –10 kg m/s.
    Rearrange the formula:
    velocity = momentum ÷ mass
            = –10 ÷ 2 *[1 mark]*
            = –5 m/s
    So recoil speed is 5 m/s *[1 mark]*.
    [Or 4 marks for the correct answer via any other method.]

Test 17: Forces
Pages 34–35
1. A *[1 mark]*   2. A *[1 mark]*
3. B *[1 mark]*   4. A *[1 mark]*
5. C *[1 mark]*   6. A *[1 mark]*
7. C *[1 mark]*   8. C *[1 mark]*
9. The object initially accelerates due to gravity *[1 mark]*. As the object's speed increases, the frictional forces on the object increase, until they match the force due to gravity and the resultant force on the object is zero *[1 mark]*. And so the object moves at terminal velocity (steady speed) *[1 mark]*.
10. pressure = force normal to surface ÷ area
    Rearrange formula:
    force normal to surface = pressure × area
    = 1.6 × 2.5 *[1 mark]*
    = 4.0 N *[1 mark]*

11. pressure due to a column of liquid = height of column × density of liquid × gravitational field strength
    $p = 1.5 \times 1000 \times 9.8$ *[1 mark]*
    = 14 700 Pa *[1 mark]*

Test 18: Forces
Pages 36–37
1. A *[1 mark]*   2. A *[1 mark]*
3. C *[1 mark]*   4. A *[1 mark]*
5. B *[1 mark]*   6. B *[1 mark]*
7. C *[1 mark]*   8. C *[1 mark]*
9. E.g.

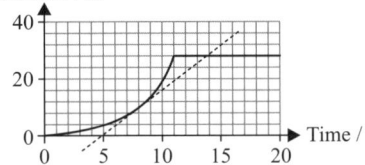

Draw a tangent at 8 s. Tangent passes through (5, 0) and (15, 32), so
change in x = 10
change in y = 32
Speed = gradient = 32 ÷ 10 = 3.2 m/s
[1 mark for drawing a tangent at 8 s, 1 mark for correctly calculated speed between 3.0 and 3.4 m/s.]

10. clockwise moment = anticlockwise moment *[1 mark]*.
    The anticlockwise moment is
    4.5 × 220 = 990 Nm *[1 mark]*, so the clockwise moment is 990 Nm. Rearrange the formula:
    distance = moment ÷ force
    = 990 ÷ 690 = 1.43...
    = 1.4 m (to 2 s.f.) *[1 mark]*
    [Or 3 marks for the correct answer via any other method.]

11. As the depth of the liquid increases, the number of particles above that point increases, so the total weight (force) acting on that point increases *[1 mark]*. Since pressure is proportional to force, the pressure in the fluid increases with depth *[1 mark]*.

Test 19: Waves
Pages 38–39
1. B *[1 mark]*   2. A *[1 mark]*
3. B *[1 mark]*   4. A *[1 mark]*
5. B *[1 mark]*   6. B *[1 mark]*
7. C *[1 mark]*   8. C *[1 mark]*

Answers

9. E.g. to cook food *[1 mark]*. Infrared waves are suitable for this purpose because they transfer energy to an object's thermal energy store when they are absorbed *[1 mark]*.
10. The electrons oscillate at the same frequency as the frequency of the absorbed wave (producing an alternating current or potential difference) *[1 mark]*.
11.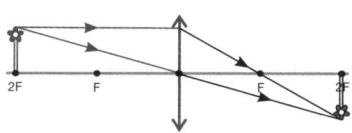

    [1 mark for correctly completed ray diagram]
    The image produced is real *[1 mark]*, inverted / upside-down *[1 mark]* and the same size as the object *[1 mark]*.

Test 20: Waves
Pages 40–41
1. A *[1 mark]*   2. C *[1 mark]*
3. A *[1 mark]*   4. B *[1 mark]*
5. B *[1 mark]*   6. B *[1 mark]*
7. B *[1 mark]*   8. A *[1 mark]*
9. wave speed = frequency × wavelength *[1 mark]*
   = $3.0 \times 10^7 \times 1.4$ *[1 mark]*
   = 4.2×10^7 m/s
   (or 42 000 000 m/s)
   [1 mark]
10. When ultrasound waves meet the boundary between two different media, they're partially reflected *[1 mark]*. A detector picks up the reflected waves *[1 mark]* and uses the timing and distribution of them to calculate how far away each boundary is and produce an image *[1 mark]*.
11. E.g.

    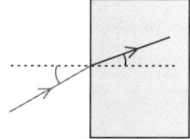

    [1 mark for a ray drawn from the point of incidence, inside the block, on the opposite side of and at a smaller angle to the normal than the incident ray].

Test 21: Waves
Pages 42–43
1. C *[1 mark]*   2. A *[1 mark]*
3. B *[1 mark]*   4. C *[1 mark]*
5. B *[1 mark]*   6. C *[1 mark]*
7. C *[1 mark]*   8. A *[1 mark]*
9. The first peak is at 0.01 s and the second peak is at 0.035 s, so:
   period = 0.035 − 0.01
   = 0.025 s *[1 mark]*
   frequency = 1 ÷ period
   = 1 ÷ 0.025 *[1 mark]*
   = 40 Hz *[1 mark]*
   [Or 3 marks for the correct answer via any other method.]
10. E.g. measure the length of a number of half-wavelengths, and divide this length by the number of half-wavelengths to find the mean half-wavelength *[1 mark]*. Double this value to find the full wavelength *[1 mark]*. Record the frequency being produced by the signal generator *[1 mark]*. Use these values and the equation 'wave speed = frequency × wavelength' to calculate the speed of the wave on the string *[1 mark]*.

Test 22: Magnetism and Electromagnetism
Pages 44–45
1. B *[1 mark]*   2. A *[1 mark]*
3. C *[1 mark]*   4. C *[1 mark]*
5. A *[1 mark]*   6. B *[1 mark]*
7. C *[1 mark]*   8. B *[1 mark]*
9. Anticlockwise *[1 mark]*.
   (To work this out, choose a side of the motor and then use Fleming's Left Hand Rule. Remember, magnetic fields go North to South.)
10. force = 176 μN = 1.76×10^{-4} N
    length = 1.1 cm = 0.011 m *[1 mark]*
    Rearrange the formula:
    magnetic field strength = $\frac{\text{force}}{\text{current} \times \text{length}}$
    = $\frac{1.76 \times 10^{-4}}{0.80 \times 0.011}$ *[1 mark]*
    magnetic field strength = 0.020 T
    [1 mark]
11. Turning a magnet inside a coil of wire induces a potential difference in the coil *[1 mark]*. As the magnet turns, the direction of potential difference across the coil changes, so an alternating potential difference is produced *[1 mark]*. If the coil is connected in a circuit, this will cause an alternating current to flow *[1 mark]*.

Test 23: Magnetism and Electromagnetism
Pages 46–47
1. A *[1 mark]*   2. B *[1 mark]*
3. B *[1 mark]*   4. C *[1 mark]*
5. A *[1 mark]*   6. A *[1 mark]*
7. B *[1 mark]*   8. B *[1 mark]*
9. N *[1 mark]*. Fleming's Left Hand Rule shows that the field goes from right to left so ? must be a north pole *[1 mark]*.
10. The compass will point north *[1 mark]*. This is because it aligns with the Earth's magnetic field / the magnetic field generated by the Earth's core *[1 mark]*.
11. potential difference across primary coil × current in primary coil
    = potential difference across secondary coil × current in secondary coil
    or $V_p I_p = V_s I_s$
    Rearrange for I_p:
    $I_p = \frac{V_s I_s}{V_p}$ *[1 mark]*
    = $\frac{400\,000 \times 0.018}{230}$ *[1 mark]*
    = 31.3... = 31 A (to 2 s.f.) *[1 mark]*

Test 24: Space Physics
Pages 48–49
1. C *[1 mark]*   2. C *[1 mark]*
3. B *[1 mark]*   4. B *[1 mark]*
5. A *[1 mark]*   6. A *[1 mark]*
7. C *[1 mark]*   8. A *[1 mark]*
9. The star remains stable because the outwards pressure caused by the energy released by nuclear fusion is balanced *[1 mark]* by the force of gravity pulling everything inwards *[1 mark]*.
10. Speed is a scalar, so it has a magnitude but not a direction. Velocity is a vector which has both a magnitude and a direction *[1 mark]*. The planet's speed remains constant but the direction of the planet's motion is constantly changing, so its velocity is changing *[1 mark]*.
11. a) The Sun *[1 mark]*
    b) The Moon/moon/natural satellite *[1 mark]*
    c) (Artificial) satellite *[1 mark]*

Test 25: Space Physics
Pages 50–51
1. A *[1 mark]*   2. C *[1 mark]*
3. A *[1 mark]*   4. A *[1 mark]*
5. B *[1 mark]*   6. A *[1 mark]*
7. C *[1 mark]*   8. C *[1 mark]*

Answers

9. a) protostar *[1 mark]*
    b) red giant *[1 mark]*
    c) black dwarf *[1 mark]*
10. When the light from a galaxy is red-shifted, it suggests that the galaxy is moving away from us *[1 mark]*. Red-shift measurements indicate that distant galaxies are moving away from us in all directions *[1 mark]*. More distant galaxies have greater red-shifts than closer ones, indicating that they are moving away faster than closer galaxies *[1 mark]*. This indicates that the whole universe is expanding, as suggested in the Big Bang theory *[1 mark]*.

Mixed Tests for Paper 2

Test 26: Paper 2 Mixed Topics
Pages 52–53

1. A *[1 mark]* 2. B *[1 mark]*
3. C *[1 mark]* 4. A *[1 mark]*
5. A *[1 mark]* 6. C *[1 mark]*
7. C *[1 mark]* 8. B *[1 mark]*
9.

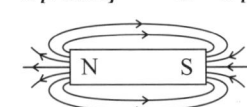

[1 mark for lines (at least 3) drawn to show the correct field shape, 1 mark for arrows drawn in correct direction on every field line.]

10. distance = speed × time, so the distance travelled by the pulse is:
    distance = $2000 \times (1 \times 10^{-5})$ *[1 mark]*
    = 0.02 m *[1 mark]*
    The ultrasound travelled to and from the boundary before it was detected, so divide the distance travelled by two to get the distance to the boundary:
    $0.02 \div 2 = 0.01$ m *[1 mark]*
11. E.g. In communication with satellites *[1 mark]*. They are suitable because they can pass through/are not absorbed by the atmosphere *[1 mark]*.

Test 27: Paper 2 Mixed Topics
Pages 54–55

1. C *[1 mark]* 2. B *[1 mark]*
3. A *[1 mark]* 4. A *[1 mark]*
5. B *[1 mark]* 6. B *[1 mark]*
7. A *[1 mark]* 8. C *[1 mark]*
9. The spring constant of the spring (in N/m) *[1 mark]*

10. The force of gravity acts inwards on the protostar, causing its temperature (and pressure) to rise *[1 mark]*. Eventually, the temperature (and the pressure) is high enough for hydrogen nuclei to undergo fusion, and the main sequence star is formed *[1 mark]*.
11. E.g. Fill the Leslie cube with boiling water *[1 mark]*. Wait for the cube to warm up, then hold a thermometer against both faces to check that they are the same temperature *[1 mark]*. Hold an infrared detector a set distance away from one of the cube's vertical faces, and record the amount of IR radiation it detects *[1 mark]*. Repeat this measurement for the other face at the same distance from the cube *[1 mark]*.

Test 28: Paper 2 Mixed Topics
Pages 56–57

1. A *[1 mark]* 2. B *[1 mark]*
3. C *[1 mark]* 4. B *[1 mark]*
5. B *[1 mark]* 6. A *[1 mark]*
7. C *[1 mark]* 8. C *[1 mark]*
9. An alternating current in the primary coil produces a changing magnetic field around the coil *[1 mark]*. This produces a changing magnetic field inside the transformer's iron core, then inside the secondary coil *[1 mark]*, which induces an alternating potential difference across the secondary coil *[1 mark]*.
10. The rod's weight acts at its centre, so the perpendicular distance of the weight from the pivot is $8 \div 2 = 4$ m *[1 mark]*.
    moment = force × perpendicular distance from the pivot
    So the clockwise moment is
    $4 \times 1500 = 6000$ Nm *[1 mark]*
    anticlockwise moment = clockwise moment *[1 mark]*
    Rearrange the formula for force:
    force = moment ÷ distance
    = $6000 \div 8 = 750$ N *[1 mark]*
    [Or 4 marks for the correct answer via any other method.]

Test 29: Paper 2 Mixed Topics
Pages 58–59

1. A *[1 mark]* 2. C *[1 mark]*
3. B *[1 mark]* 4. B *[1 mark]*
5. A *[1 mark]* 6. C *[1 mark]*
7. C *[1 mark]* 8. B *[1 mark]*

9. Rearrange the formula:
   object height
   = image height ÷ magnification
   = $13.5 \div 3$ *[1 mark]*
   = 4.5 cm *[1 mark]*
10. The card has a rougher surface than the mirror, so the beam reflected from the card will be wider and dimmer (diffuse reflection) *[1 mark]* than the beam reflected from the mirror, which will be thin and bright (specular reflection) *[1 mark]*.
11. The distance is equal to the area under the graph. Area under the graph from 0 s to 10 s is:
    $0.5 \times 10 \times 80 = 400$ m *[1 mark]*
    and area from 10 s to 15 s is
    $5 \times 80 = 400$ m *[1 mark]*
    so the distance travelled is
    $400 + 400 = 800$ m *[1 mark]*
    [Or 3 marks for the correct answer via any other method.]

Test 30: Paper 2 Mixed Topics
Pages 60–61

1. C *[1 mark]* 2. B *[1 mark]*
3. A *[1 mark]* 4. B *[1 mark]*
5. C *[1 mark]* 6. C *[1 mark]*
7. A *[1 mark]* 8. A *[1 mark]*
9. The measured distance covers 5 wavelengths, so
   wavelength = $42 \div 5$
   = 8.4 cm *[1 mark]* = 0.084 m
   wave speed = frequency × wavelength
   = 4.0×0.084 *[1 mark]*
   = 0.336 m/s
   = 0.34 m/s (to 2 s.f) *[1 mark]*
   [Or 3 marks for the correct answer via any other method.]
10. E.g. using scale 1 cm = 10 N

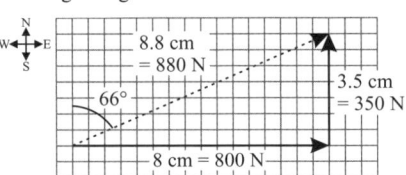

Magnitude = 880 N
Direction = 66° from north
[1 mark for drawing vertical force and horizontal force correctly, 1 mark for drawing resultant force correctly, 1 mark for giving magnitude of force between 870 and 890 N and 1 mark for giving direction between 65° and 67°.]